Jehovah Rapha

30-DAY JOURNAL

This Journal Belongs to:

_____

Copyright © 2019 Rebecca Love, All rights reserved.

All Scripture quotations, unless otherwise indicated, are taken from The Holy Bible, King James Version®

www.gumroad.com/jehovarapha
ISBN: 978-1692995836

Jehovah Rapha
30-DAY JOURNAL

It is good to write down your thoughts, scriptures, prayers, what God has done in your life, etc. God made you to be you. So allow your personality to come out.

Each day begin by reading the scripture and after you read the prompt pray about whatever comes to mind and then begin to write. It doesn't matter what you put in your journal. What does matter is that you are in conversation with the Father.

Keeping a journal is a simple, delightful way to spend time with the God who loves you!

- Minister Rebecca Love

Day One

See now that I, even I, am he, and there is no god with me: I kill, and I make alive; I wound, and I heal: neither is there any that can deliver out of my hand.

Deuteronomy 32:39

Date_____

What is God offering to be and do for you?

Day Two

O LORD my God, I cried unto thee, and thou hast healed me.

Psalm 30:2

Date_____

Do you believe your cry has been heard?

Day Three

He sent his word, and healed them, and delivered them from their destructions.

Psalm 107:20

Date_____

Have you been in a dangerous situation and a Word came from God?

Day Four

Heal me, O LORD, *and I shall be healed; save me, and I shall be saved: for thou art my praise.*

Jeremiah 17:14

Date_____

What are you petitioning God for?

Day Five

And Jesus saith unto him, I will come and heal him.

Matthew 8:7

Date_____

Jesus did go and heal him. Do you want Him to heal you?

Day Six

And Jesus went about all Galilee, teaching in their synagogues, and preaching the gospel of the kingdom, and healing all manner of sickness and all manner of disease among the people.

Matthew 4:23

Date_____

Are there any limitations on the healing Jesus provides? Name a few illnesses you would like Jesus to heal

_____
_____
_____
_____
_____
_____
_____
_____
_____
_____
_____
_____
_____
_____

Day Seven

When the even was come, they brought unto him many that were possessed with devils: and he cast out the spirits with his word, and healed all that were sick:

Matthew 8:16

Date_____

Jesus healed all manner of diseases, how did He do it?

Day Eight

Heal the sick, cleanse the lepers, raise the dead, cast out devils: freely ye have received, freely give.

Matthew 10:8

Date_____

Is there a cost for healing? How would you pay? What would you pay?

Day Nine

And whithersoever he entered, into villages, or cities, or country, they laid the sick in the streets, and besought him that they might touch if it were but the border of his garment: and as many as touched him were made whole.

Mark 6:56

*Date*_____

Where have you laid?

___
___
___
___
___
___
___
___
___
___
___
___
___
___
___
___
___
___
___
___
___

Day Ten

Who forgiveth all thine iniquities; who healeth all thy diseases;

Psalm 103:3

Date_____

How many diseases did He heal? Are there any illnesses you would like to ask Him to heal?

_____
_____
_____
_____
_____
_____
_____
_____
_____
_____
_____
_____

Day Eleven

I create the fruit of the lips; Peace, peace to him that is far off, and to him that is near, saith the LORD; *and I will heal him.*

Isaiah 57:19

Date_____

What did He do? How can He heal you?

Day Twelve

And Jesus went forth, and saw a great multitude, and was moved with compassion toward them, and he healed their sick.

Matthew 14:14

Date_____

How can you help someone that needs healing?

Day Thirteen

Now when the sun was setting, all they that had any sick with divers diseases brought them unto him; and he laid his hands on every one of them, and healed them.

Luke 4:40

Date_____

What time of day was it that Jesus laid hands on them? How many were healed?

Day Fourteen

And when he had called unto him his twelve disciples, he gave them power against unclean spirits, to cast them out, and to heal all manner of sickness and all manner of disease.

Matthew 10:1

Date_____

He gave power to His disciples, to do what?

Day Fifteen

And he went forth unto the spring of the waters, and cast the salt in there, and said, Thus saith the Lord, I have healed these waters; there shall not be from thence any more death or barren land.

2 Kings 2:21

Date_____

What was wrong with the water?

Day Sixteen

The Spirit of the Lord is upon me, because he hath anointed me to preach the gospel to the poor; he hath sent me to heal the brokenhearted, to preach deliverance to the captives, and recovering of sight to the blind, to set at liberty them that are bruised,

Luke 4:18

Date_____

Sickness is satanic bondage. God wants you healed, can you name something you can do?

_____
_____
_____
_____
_____
_____
_____
_____
_____
_____
_____
_____
_____
_____
_____
_____

Day Seventeen

By stretching forth thine hand to heal; and that signs and wonders may be done by the name of thy holy child Jesus.

Acts 4:30

Date_____

Who heals signs and wonders, and in what name?

Day Eighteen

How God anointed Jesus of Nazareth with the Holy Ghost and with power: who went about doing good, and healing all that were oppressed of the devil; for God was with him.

Acts 10:38

Date_____

Who anointed Jesus? What was He anointed with? Who was with Him?

Day Nineteen

To another faith by the same Spirit; to another the gifts of healing by the same Spirit.

1Corinthians 12:9

Date_____

Is healing a gift?

Day Twenty

Confess your faults one to another, and pray one for another, that ye may be healed. The effectual fervent prayer of a righteous man availeth much.

James 5:16

Date_____

Why should we confess one to another?
Why should we pray for one another?

Day Twenty-One

Who his own self bare our sins in his own body on the tree, that we, being dead to sins, should live unto righteousness: by whose stripes ye were healed.

1 Peter 2:24

Date_____

He was wounded for who and why?

Day Twenty-Two

If my people, which are called by my name, shall humble themselves, and pray, and seek my face, and turn from their wicked ways; then will I hear from heaven, and will forgive their sin, and will heal their land.

2 Chronicles 7:14

Date_____

What can you do to heal the land?

Day Twenty-Three

He healeth the broken in heart, and bindeth up their wounds.

Psalm 147:3

Date_____

Are you experiencing a time in your life that your heart needs mending?

___

Day Twenty-Four

Then Jesus answered and said unto her, O woman, great is thy faith: be it unto thee even as thou wilt. And her daughter was made whole from that very hour.

Matthew 15:28

Date_____

Pray for your children...

Day Twenty-Five

And they that were vexed with unclean spirits: and they were healed.

Luke 6:18

Date_____

Where are the people coming from and why?

Day Twenty-Six

And the blind and the lame came to him in the temple; and he healed them.

Matthew 21:14

Date_____

Describe the need of the people. Who did they go to and why?

___
___
___
___
___
___
___
___
___
___
___
___
___
___
___
___
___
___

Day Twenty-Seven

And he said unto her, Daughter, thy faith hath made thee whole; go in peace, and be whole of thy plague.

Mark 5:34

Date_____

Are you whole? What do you need to touch Jesus about?

_____
_____
_____
_____
_____
_____
_____
_____
_____
_____
_____
_____
_____
_____
_____
_____

Day Twenty-Eight

The centurion answered and said, Lord, I am not worthy that thou shouldest come under my roof: but speak the word only, and my servant shall be healed.

Matthew 8:8

Date_____

Why did the Centurion feel unworthy? What are some things you need Jesus to do for you?

Day Twenty-Nine

Have mercy upon me, O LORD; *for I am weak:* O LORD, *heal me; for my bones are vexed.*

Psalms 6:2

Date_____

Have you ever felt like no matter what you do there has been no change in your area of illness?

_____
_____
_____
_____
_____
_____
_____
_____
_____
_____
_____
_____
_____
_____
_____
_____

Day Thirty

Return, ye backsliding children, and I will heal your backslidings. Behold, we come unto thee; for thou art the LORD our God.

Jeremiah 3:22

Date_____

Is disobedience holding up your healing?

Your Personal Reflections

ABOUT THE CREATOR

Minister Rebecca Love *is known for her love for evangelizing, preaching and praying. She received her license to preach the gospel in October 2005 under the leadership of Bishop L. Kirby and First Lady Dr. R. Sartan Kirby of St. Paul MB Church.*

Minister Rebecca is encouraged to be an encouragement to God's people as well as a helping hand. She believes that Jesus Christ is the reason for living and in His mercy and Grace we shall live unto God and not ourselves.

God bless you richly.

Minister Rebecca Love

Connect with Minister Rebecca

Email: loverebecca58@yahoo.com